WELCOME TO THE WORLD OF

Eagles

Diane Swanson

Whitecap Books
Vancouver / Toronto

The information in this book is true and complete to the best of our knowledge.
All recommendations are made without guarantee on the part of the author or
Whitecap Books. The author and publisher disclaim any liability in connection
with the use of this information. For additional information please contact
Whitecap Books, 351 Lynn Avenue, North Vancouver, BC V7J 2C4.

Edited by Elizabeth McLean
Cover design by Steve Penner
Cover photograph by Thomas Kitchin/First Light
Interior design by Margaret Ng
Typeset by Tanya Lloyd
Photo credits: Thomas Kitchin/First Light iv, 18; Tim Christie 2; Wayne Lynch 4,
22, 24; Lynn M. Stone 6, 8, 10, 14, 16, 20, 26; S. Osolinski/First Light 12

Printed and bound in Canada

Canadian Cataloguing in Publication Data

Swanson, Diane, 1944–
    Welcome to the world of eagles

    Includes index.
    ISBN 1-55110-706-6

    1. Eagles—North America—Juvenile literature. I. Title.
QL696.F32S92 1998   j598.9'42   C98-910009-X

For more information on
this series and other
Whitecap Books titles,
visit our web site at
www.whitecap.ca

The publisher acknowledges the support of the Canada Council for the Arts for
our publishing program and the Cultural Services Branch of the Government of
British Columbia in making this publication possible.

Contents

World of Difference   1

Where in the World   5

World of the Hunter   9

World of Words   13

World of Mates   17

New World   21

Fun World   25

Index   28

World of Difference

LOOK UP HIGH TO SEE EAGLES IN THE SKY. With strong wings beating deeply, they take off into the wind. They rise higher and higher, then hold their wings steady and g-l-i-d-e.

Eagles catch rides on big bubbles of rising air. The birds spiral up and up until they disappear from sight. Then they swoop down and ride back up again.

The eagle is one of the biggest birds on Earth. With wings outstretched, it could easily span the length of your bed. But it usually weighs no more than a small dog— about 6 kilograms (13 pounds).

A master of flight, the bald eagle seems to rule the sky.

1

A black tip marks the thick beak of the golden eagle.

Around the world, there are about 60 different kinds of eagles. In North America, there are just 2 kinds: golden eagles and bald eagles. Both were named for the color of feathers on their necks and heads. "White" is one meaning of the word "bald."

Worldwide, golden eagles belong to a group of booted eagles. Unlike other kinds, their legs and feet are covered with feathers. Bald eagles belong to a group of fishing eagles. The bottoms of their feet are rough, making it easier to hold onto slippery fish.

All eagles feed on meat. Both golden and bald eagles have strong feet as large as a man's hands. They have hooked claws—called talons—for nabbing and killing prey. And they have curved, pointed beaks for tearing flesh.

POWER POLE EAGLES

Eagles sometimes perch on poles instead of trees. But many poles are strung with wires that carry a lot of electricity. If an eagle's wings touch two of these wires at once: ZAP! Electricity flows through its body, usually killing the bird—especially if its wings are wet.

People have worked to make power poles safer. Some put up landing bars so eagles can perch above the wires. Some set up barriers so that eagles can't perch between the wires.

3

Where in the World

EAGLES LIVE WHERE EAGLES EAT. Bald eagles usually live close to water because fish is their main food. They hunt along oceans, lakes, and rivers.

Golden eagles eat almost any prey they can, so they hunt almost anywhere: in mountains, open forests, grasslands, and deserts. But they seem to prefer hilly over flat land, where they can easily grab rides on rising air.

Both kinds of eagles have territories—areas where they live and hunt. They guard their territories from other eagles, even attacking invaders if they must.

High places, like a branch on this tall tree in Florida, make good lookouts for eagles.

5

Wintry weather doesn't bother bald eagles as long as the rivers still flow with fish.

When eagles rest or nest, they head for tree branches or ledges on rocky cliffs. Some even perch on poles. But if there are no trees, cliffs, or poles around, they may just settle on the ground.

In spring and fall, many eagles head for new places to feed. Some fly south for the winter, where it's easier to find food. But in the warm state of Florida, for example, adult bald eagles usually stay put all year.

Except for Antarctica, every continent is home to eagles of one kind or another. In years past, there were more eagles than there are now, and they lived in more places. Today, bald eagles still fly in North America, but most live along the northwest coast. Golden eagles live across most of Canada, in the western United States, and in parts of Mexico, Europe, Asia, and Africa.

GOLDEN JOURNEY

In 1992, a bird watcher in Canada discovered the world's longest flight path for golden eagles. Each fall, up to 10,000 golden eagles fly south along the Rocky Mountains as far as Mexico. Then in spring, they head north as far as the Arctic.

Traveling up to 700 kilometres (435 miles) a day, the eagles save energy by spiraling on air bubbles above the mountain peaks, then gliding down. They may glide a long, long way before they spiral up again.

World of the Hunter

IT'S EASY FOR EAGLES TO HUNT. From high up, their sharp eyes can spot fish in the water and mice on the ground. And eagles have all the tools they need to catch their prey.

With wings folded back, the eagle dives on its target. As it's about to strike, its feet swing forward. Toes with razor-sharp talons nab the prey. One blow from the talon on the back toe is usually enough to kill.

The eagle often flies to a perch to eat its catch—unless it's too heavy to carry. With its sharp beak, the eagle may strip off fur or feathers before ripping its meal apart.

Swoop. Snatch. This bald eagle has a fish for dinner.

Although the beak gets worn down by plenty of hard use, it never wears out. Like the eagle's talons, it keeps growing as long as the eagle lives—up to 25 years.

Bald eagles often wade into shallow water to grab dead fish. They also swoop down and snatch up live fish, sometimes plunging right into the water.

A young bald eagle — feathered in colors different from an adult's — is a keen fisher.

If they get too wet to fly off, they swim back to shore, paddling with their wings.

Besides fish, bald eagles also eat some of the same food that golden eagles eat: rabbits, rats, snakes, turtles— even garbage. They may also attack young wolves, deer, and sheep.

Eagles mostly hunt alone, but sometimes they work in pairs. One might scare prey out of hiding, while the other attacks it. Or the eagles might just steal dinner from other birds.

DANGER: FALLING FOOD!

A story from ancient Greece told of a poet who was warned: "Be careful! A house may fall and kill you." All day, the poet stayed away from buildings.

A flying eagle mistook the poet's bald head for a large stone and dropped a turtle on it. Sure enough, the blow from the turtle's "house"—its hard shell— killed the poet. Eagles often drop animals such as turtles and clams to crack open their shells. Then they can eat the soft insides.

11

World of Words

EAGLE EGGS CHIRP. THEN EAGLE MOTHERS CHIRP BACK. They know that the eaglets are almost ready to break out of their eggs. But soon after the eaglets hatch, their chirps turn to squawks as they holler for food.

Like other animals, eagles talk to each other by making different calls and by moving their bodies different ways. Golden eagles, which spend most of their time alone, have less to say than bald eagles. But both kinds call out as they court their mates, spot other eagles in their territories, and guard their food.

Bald eagles use their hearing more when talking than when hunting.

13

The golden eagle is making a threat: "Stay away from my prey."

To say, "Don't eat my lunch," the eagles stare hard, fluff out their feathers, and scream. Their message is especially clear if they are standing on top of their food at the time.

When eagles soar through the sky, they seldom talk at all. But as they approach their nests, bald eagles make squeaky noises, over and over again. They seem to be announcing, "Here I come." Golden eagles may make yelping noises near their nests, mainly when they are bringing home food.

If an eagle has been tending its eggs for quite a while, it may cry to its mate. That means, "Let's trade places." It may also dive at its mate to be sure the mate understands.

But it's easiest for eagles to say, "I'm hot." Like a dog, the eagle just lets its mouth hang open. Then it dangles its tongue, and pants.

GATHERING, BLATHERING

"Keeree-ree-ik-ik-ik-ik," scream the eagles in the trees. "Keeree-ree-ik-ik-ik-ik," scream the eagles on the ground. All this blathering goes on between bites of dinner. It grows loudest when eagles get close to each other.

Each fall, thousands of bald eagles gather and blather loudly along a few rivers that flow thick with salmon. After the fish deposit and fertilize their eggs, they die—and become good eagle food.

15

World of Mates

EAGLES TAKE THEIR MATES SKY DANCING. Together, a couple soars, swoops, glides, and dives through the air. One eagle may follow the other. Or one may swoop down while the other soars up. At times, the lower bird flips over so its talons can reach those of the higher bird. The two may even grip each other's toes and cartwheel down together—almost to the ground.

For both golden and bald eagles, the bond between mates usually lasts a lifetime. And each year, they return to the same place—often to the same

A quiet moment is one of many things eagle mates share.

nest—to raise their families.

Both kinds of eagles prefer nests in tall trees or on ledges along steep cliffs. High-up places make the best lookouts. Bald eagles like nests close to water, where they hunt.

The couple often works together to build a big nest of branches and sticks. If the eagles reuse a nest, they enlarge it first

Home sweet home for a bald eagle is a gigantic nest, built high in a tree.

and reline it with grass, moss, and pine needles. Bald eagles sometimes add seaweed. Then the nest is ready to cradle their eggs. The female usually lays two eggs in the spring. Both mates warm them and keep them safe.

Few eagles mind having guests in their nests. Small birds such as house sparrows sometimes make homes on the outside of a nest while eagles are inside. And after the eagles move out, their nest may become home to other guests: owls, squirrels, or raccoons.

People who build eagle nests soon discover how huge they are. At one nursery school, 14 children gathered sticks to make a bald eagle nest—just for fun. Together, they formed a line that reached only halfway around the nest.

After a storm knocked down one bald eagle's nest, people rebuilt it. They wove sticks into a wire frame and lined it with grass. It was three times deeper than a bathtub, and it weighed 90 kilograms (200 pounds).

New World

BREAKING OUT OF AN EGG TAKES HOURS OF WORK. So an eaglet is ready to eat soon after it hatches. Its mother feeds it tiny bits of flesh, torn from prey that its father catches.

At first, the mother stays close to the eaglet, often keeping it under her wing. She makes sure it's not too cold and not too hot. She protects it from other animals, such as owls. But before very long, she leaves it alone for a while as she helps her mate hunt.

When the eaglet is a few weeks old, the mother eagle brings food to the nest—but

Mealtime comes often for the bald eaglets in this ground nest in Alaska.

21

starts to eat it herself. The hungry eaglet SCREAMS and SQUAWKS. Then it drapes its wings over the food and tears off bits. It learns to feed itself.

As its wings get stronger, the eaglet flaps them a lot. Sometimes it flaps so much that the eaglet lifts up off its feet. Day by day, the little bird

A golden eaglet changes its coat from white, fuzzy down to dark feathers.

rises higher above the nest.

Soon the eaglet is flying, and it's ready to learn how to hunt. It watches its parents grab a snake, a fish—even a lamb. And it tries to do the same.

At first, the eaglet misses its prey, but it gradually improves. It even learns to steal food from crows and other eagles, just as its parents do.

By fall, the eaglet is ready to find its own food and, years later, its own mate. It's ready to be part of a much bigger world.

FLYING LESSONS

Teaching an eaglet to fly takes time. A parent eagle may circle its nest, clutching a fish. That makes the eaglet in the nest squawk and flap its wings. The parent keeps circling and flying off until the eaglet chases the fish.

The eaglet flies as far as it can before landing. As it rests, the parent eagle feeds it the fish. Then both birds return to the nest. Each day, the parent draws the eaglet farther until it learns to fly well.

Fun World

YOUNG EAGLES ARE EAGER FOR FUN. They start playing when they're only four or five weeks old. Their nest becomes their playpen.

At first, the eaglets just crawl around, exploring the nest. As they grow bigger and stronger, they start hopping about. And when they're able to flap their wings hard, the eaglets can rise above the nest. Up and down they go—like children jumping on a trampoline.

Eaglets have plenty of toys: feathers, twigs, leaves, bones, fish heads, scraps of fur, and bits of leftover food. Playing alone,

A webbed foot? A tail? Which toys will these golden eaglets play with next?

25

an eaglet tosses its toys around with its beak. It heaves them into the air, then grabs them when they land in the nest. It attacks them as if they were prey. Sometimes the eaglet uses its beak to catch and crush the toys. Other times, it uses its talons and toes to pounce on the toys or snatch them.

"That was fun," this bald eagle seems to say after pouncing on some white feathers.

If there are two eaglets in a family, they will play together. When one flings a toy, they both try to grab it. If they snatch the toy at the same time, the game may change to tug-of-war. All their romping and stomping usually flattens out the nest.

It's lucky that eaglets spend so much time playing. It gives them plenty of exercise. It helps them get ready to fly, and it gives them practice hunting. All that fun helps to make life as a full-grown eagle a little easier.

EAGLE WONDERS

Eagles are amazing! Here are some of the reasons why:

- Extra, see-through eyelids protect eagle eyes from dust, rain, and bright light.
- Eagles can kill prey four times heavier than themselves.
- One 36-year-old bald eagle nest in the United States weighed as much as a minivan.
- When they build nests, eagles may use some rabbit bones as twigs.

Index

Africa 7
Age 10
Alaska 21
Antarctica 7
Arctic 7
Asia 7

Bald eagles 1, 2, 3, 5, 6,
    7, 9, 10–11, 13, 14–15,
    17–18, 19, 21, 26
Birds 1, 11, 19, 21, 23
Booted eagles 2–3

Canada 7
Color 2, 10, 22

Eaglets 13, 21–23, 25–27
Eggs 13, 15, 19, 21
Enemies 21
Europe 7

Families 18, 21–23, 27
Feeding 3, 6, 9, 11, 15,
    21–22, 23
Fish 3, 5, 6, 9, 10, 11,
    15, 23, 25

Fishing eagles 3
Florida 5, 7
Flying 1, 5, 7, 11, 14, 17,
    22–23, 25, 27

Golden eagles 2–3, 5, 7,
    11, 13, 14, 15, 17–18,
    22, 25
Greece 11
Guarding 5, 13, 19, 21

Hatching 13, 21
Hearing 13
Homes 5–7, 17–19, 21,
    27
Hunting 5, 9–11, 18, 21,
    23, 27

Mates 13, 15, 17–19, 21,
    23
Mexico 7

Nests 6, 14, 15, 18–19,
    21, 23, 25, 26, 27
North America 2, 7

People 3, 11, 19
Playing 25–27
Population 7
Prey 3, 5, 9, 11, 14, 21,
    23, 27

Rabbits 11, 27
Rocky Mountains 7

Senses 9, 27
Sight 9, 27
Size 1, 3
Snakes 11, 23

Talking 13–15, 22, 23
Teaching 21–22, 23
Territories 5, 13
Traveling 6, 7, 17–18

United States 7, 27

Weight 1